Amazing Nature

Pesky Parasites

John Woodward

Heinemann Library
Chicago, Illinois

Customer Service 888-454-2279
Visit our website at www.heinemannlibrary.com

Produced for Heinemann Library by Discovery Books Limited
Originated by Ambassador Litho Ltd
Printed in China by South China Printing Company

08 07 06 05 04
10 9 8 7 6 5 4 3 2 1

Library of Congress Cataloging-in-Publication Data
Woodward, John, 1954-
  Pesky parasites / John Woodward.
      p. cm. -- (Amazing nature)
Summary: Introduces a variety of animals and plants that live off of other living beings in a parsite/host relationship, including the flea, ghost orchid, and tapeworm.
Includes bibliographical references (p.   ) and index.
  ISBN 1-4034-4707-1 -- ISBN 1-4034-5403-5 (pbk.)
  1. Parasites--Juvenile literature. 2. Parasitic plants--Juvenile literature. [1. Parasites. 2. Parasitic plants.] I. Title. II. Series.
  QL757.W655 2003
  577.8'57--dc22

                              2003022043

Acknowledgments
The publisher would like to thank the following for permission to reproduce photographs:
pp. 4, 27 David Hosking/FLPA; p. 5 Joan Hutchings/FLPA; p. 6 Kim Taylor/Bruce Coleman Collection; p. 7A Alastair MacEwen/Oxford Scientific Films; p. 7B Linda Pitkin/Natural History Photographic Agency; p. 8 G. E. Hyde/FLPA; p. 9 Zig Leszczynski/AA/Oxford Scientific Films; p. 10 R. Planck/Dembinsky/FLPA; p. 11 Daniel Heuclin/Natural History Photographic Agency; p. 12 London Scientific Films/Oxford Scientific Films; p. 13 Roger Tidman/FLPA; pp. 14, 17, 28 Breck P. Kent/AA/Oxford Scientific Films; p. 15 Ron Boardman/Life Science Ima/FLPA; pp. 16, 22B Tony Wharton/FLPA; p. 18 Jeremy Thomas/Natural Visions; p. 19 Peter David/Natural Visions; p. 20 S. Maslowski/FLPA; p. 21 Maurice Walker/FLPA; p. 22A Tom Leach/Oxford Scientific Films; p. 23 Ian Rose/FLPA; p. 24A K. G. Preston-Mafham/Premaphotos; p. 24B Jurgen & Christine Sohns/FLPA; p. 25 James H. Robinson/Oxford Scientific Films; p. 26 Martin Harvey/Natural History Photographic Agency; p. 29 Image Quest 3-D.

Cover photograph of a human flea: Paulo De Oliveira/Oxford Scientific Films.

Some words are shown in bold, **like this.** You can find out what they mean by looking in the glossary.

Contents

Living Lunch

All living things need food. Green plants can make their own food out of air and water. But most other living things, including all animals, have to find food that is already made. They do this by eating other living things.

Many animals eat plants and animals that are already dead. Others attack animals that are alive. Then, they kill them by eating them or kill them and then eat them. But some living things are experts at feeding on living animals. The animals that do this are called **parasites**.

Some of the most famous parasites are leeches. They use suckers to attach themselves to other animals, including humans, and suck their blood.

*Mistletoe is a plant that grows on trees and steals sugary **sap** from them. But it never steals enough to kill the trees, since this would leave it without a home.*

A true parasite steals all its food from another living thing, called its **host,** and gives nothing back. A parasite might attach itself to the outside of another animal or plant, or even live inside it. Life for a parasite can be dangerous, especially for those that cling to the outside of animals with sharp claws. But parasites that live inside other animals are warm, safe, and surrounded by food.

Killing a host

A true parasite feeds off its host, but it never takes too much. It wants to keep its host alive because if the host dies, the parasite often dies too. Some **insect** parasites, however, eat their hosts alive and finally kill them. Others are bloodsuckers that attack many different victims. Some of these bloodsuckers carry very tiny parasites inside their own bodies. The parasites can cause deadly diseases.

Leaping and Creeping

Fleas and lice are tiny **insect parasites** that live among the fur and hair of bigger animals. They have mouthparts like needles that they use to stab their victims and suck their blood. Some fleas and lice can carry diseases, but most do not cause any serious harm.

There are at least 2,000 different kinds of fleas, and each has its own favorite **host**. One flea prefers cats, but it will bite other animals too, including humans. Like all fleas, it has a very narrow body so it can move between hairs easily. It also has rows of bristles on its body that catch in the cat's fur and help the flea hold on tight.

Cat fleas live in cat fur. The fleas feed on cats, but they jump off to breed in carpets. The next thing they jump on might be you!

Fleas are famous for the way they jump. A flea's back legs contain a rubbery substance that works like springs. The springs are pulled tight by powerful muscles, then released with a snap to fling the flea into the air. A cat flea can jump 250 times its own length.

Crawling and gripping

Lice do not jump. They just cling to hair or fur with their strong claws and move around by crawling. Lice can crawl from one host to another, but only if their victims are close together. Each type of louse has claws that are good only for gripping certain types of hair. Human head lice, the kind you might pick up at school, can only live in human hair.

The last meal of human blood stolen by this human head louse can be clearly seen through its transparent body.

Louse links

Even fish suffer from lice. But these lice are not insects. They are more like tiny crabs or wood lice that cling to the scaly skins of their hosts and suck their blood.

There is nothing that this tropical coral reef fish can do about the fish louse sucking its blood.

Visiting Vampires

Lice and fleas usually cling to their **hosts** for awhile, but other bloodsucking **parasites** just make quick visits when they are hungry. They often attack in the dark, steal some blood, and disappear.

One of these parasites is the bedbug. This small, flat, reddish-brown **insect** really does live in beds, but is also found in cracks in walls, door frames and old furniture. It creeps out in the middle of the night and sniffs its way toward a sleeping human. It slips its very sharp, thin beak into the human's skin and starts to suck. By the time the bedbug has finished and crept away, its body is swollen with blood. The bedbug's victim wakes up with an itchy bump.

Hungry bedbugs have flattened bodies so they can slip into narrow cracks and hide during the day, but they get much fatter when they feed.

Luckily, bedbugs do not carry any nasty diseases, but the much bigger Chagas bug of South America can. It feeds in the same way as the bedbug, but inside of it is a parasite of its own that causes an infection called Chagas' disease. About half a million people get Chagas' disease every year, and 50,000 die within twelve weeks of catching it.

A vampire bat often uses its wings as front legs, running and jumping over the ground to get at its victims.

Vampires in the night

South America is also the home of the vampire bat. A vampire bat may attack sleeping people, but it prefers cattle and similar animals. The bat slices into their skin with its razor-sharp teeth and laps up their blood with its tongue. The vampire bats do not take much blood, but some carry rabies, a dangerous disease that can kill.

Disease Carriers

The most dangerous of all bloodsuckers are the flies we call mosquitoes. Only the females drink blood, which they need to make their eggs. A mosquito's mouthparts are shaped like a very fine, sharp, hollow needle. She slips this needle into an animal's skin without being noticed. A mosquito takes very little blood, and usually it leaves only an itchy bump. The itch is caused by the mosquito's **saliva,** which it pumps into the wound to keep the blood flowing. But the saliva of some mosquitoes contains very tiny **parasites** that can cause deadly diseases.

This mosquito's body is swollen with blood that she has sucked from her victim's hand.

Terrible ticks

Many people think spiders are scary, but spiders have some small relatives called ticks that are much scarier. Ticks look like tiny crabs. They sit on twigs and grass, waiting for an animal to pass by. If one does, the tick will hop on its skin, punch a hole with its sharp, beak-like mouthparts and start sucking its blood. It sticks itself to the skin with a kind of natural glue. If the victim tries to pull the tick off while it is drinking, the tick's front half still hangs on. As it drinks, the tick's body swells up. It drinks up to 500 times its own body weight of blood and then drops off to lay its eggs.

Ticks are dangerous because very tiny parasites can be carried in their saliva. The parasites are injected into the blood of their victims and can cause terrible diseases. These diseases can be treated by medicine, and if caught early they are easily cured. This is good, because two of the worst diseases, Rocky Mountain spotted fever and Colorado tick fever, can kill the victim if they are not treated. Another, Lyme disease, causes a rash, flu-like symptoms, and heart problems. Lyme disease can kill its victims.

This deer tick, blown up like a shiny bean with all the blood it has stolen, may have given its victim a nasty disease.

Ticks have some even smaller relatives called mites. They include the scabies or itch mite, which burrows under its victim's skin to feed. It causes such terrible itching that its victims often scratch themselves raw.

Munching maggots

Many flies lay their eggs on dead animals. The **maggots** that hatch from the eggs eat the meat of those animals, and they do a good job getting rid of dead bodies. Some flies, however, lay their eggs on live animals. The warble fly, for example, glues its eggs to the legs of cattle and deer. When the eggs hatch, the maggots burrow under their **host's** skin. They gradually eat their way to the animal's back and settle in painful swellings called warbles. After a few months they burst out and fall to the ground, where they become adult warble flies. The holes in the host animal's skin heal once the maggots have gone.

A warble fly has found a host for its eggs. Cattle have learned to recognize the buzz of a warble fly, and even run away across the fields to escape from it.

The horse botfly is even worse. Horses lick their own skin, and the fly lays its eggs where they will be licked up into the horse's mouth. The maggots hatch in the horse's mouth, then travel down to its stomach where they feed on its insides, causing nasty **ulcers**.

The horse botfly spends most of its life as a maggot inside a horse. When it becomes an adult, it lives just long enough to lay its eggs.

The most interesting of these parasitic flies is the human botfly of Central and South America. Instead of laying its egg on someone's skin, it attaches the egg to a mosquito. When the mosquito bites someone, the egg quickly hatches and the tiny maggot dives into the hole left by the bite. It anchors itself with rings of stiff bristles and starts eating the victim's flesh. As it grows, the botfly maggot begins to itch, then hurt. When it grows to about 1 inch (25 millimeters) long, it falls out and turns into an adult fly.

Invading Worms

Some **parasites** spend their entire lives inside other animals. They steal everything they need from their **hosts,** including all their food and water. They do not even have to breathe. Most of these invaders are worms. Some are tiny, like the whipworms that live in pigs and in uncooked pork. One mouthful of uncooked pork can contain a million tiny young worms. They grow and multiply inside the human body and spread out to feed on the muscles, heart, lungs, eyes, and even the brain. Any infected person can become very sick.

Other worms are bigger. Roundworms look a bit like smooth, colorless earthworms. They live inside the **intestines** of other animals, eating their food. One type of roundworm that attacks humans can produce about 200,000 eggs a day. These eggs get scattered in **feces**. If you swallow some of the eggs by mistake they hatch inside you. The worms can grow to over 12 inches (30 centimeters) long.

This is a roundworm taken from a pig. If raw feces from farm animals are used as fertilizer on fields, roundworm eggs can get on farm crops. The eggs can hatch inside people's stomachs when they eat the crops.

The biggest insiders are tapeworms. The beef tapeworm, which spends its early life in the flesh of a cow, can grow to an amazing 26 feet (8 meters) long. It can grow inside the intestine of a human who has eaten some raw meat with a young tapeworm in it. The tapeworm spends the rest of its life inside its human host, producing millions of eggs that leave the human body in feces.

This is just the head of a beef tapeworm. It uses its crown of hooks like an anchor to grip the inside of its host's intestine.

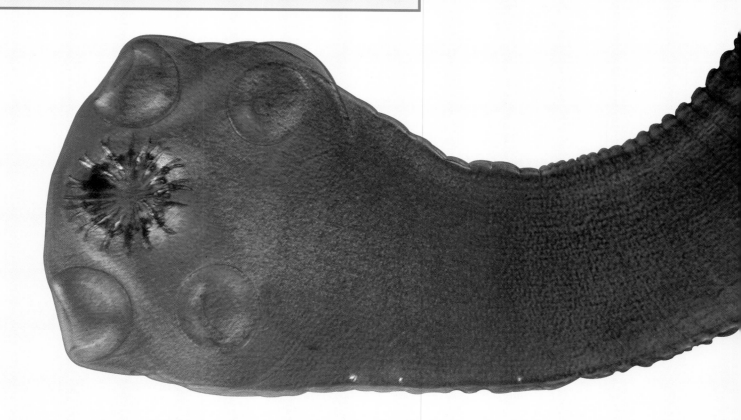

The worm parasites that live inside humans are not a problem in countries that have proper water supplies and food inspectors. People are only infected with them when they drink dirty water or eat food that has not been properly cooked. Cooking destroys all the worms that could otherwise make their home inside you.

Murderous Wasps

Most **parasites** try not to kill their **hosts**. They need their hosts to be alive to make sure they get their food. But many parasitic **insect larvae** called **parasitoids** (pear-uh-sih-toyds) keep eating until their host dies. Then they turn into winged insects and fly away.

The real experts at this are wasps: not the striped, stinging kind that breed in buzzing nests, but slender insects that live alone. They include the ichneumon (ick-nyoo-mun) wasps. These wasps look for fat insect larvae that eat their way through wood.

A female ichneumon lays her eggs through a long tube. The tube works like a drill, but it is no wider than a single hair. Amazingly, the tip of this drill is hardened with metal that the wasp has picked up from the plants it eats. This metal tip allows the wasp to drill through the wood to the insect larva. The wasp lays a tiny egg through the tube. When the wasp egg hatches into a larva, it eats its victim alive.

You can just see the long, thin drill of this ichneumon wasp as she bores into a branch to lay an egg on her victim—an insect larva.

The much bigger tarantula hawk wasp attacks giant, hairy tarantula spiders. It stings a spider to **paralyze** it, then lays an egg on the spider's body and buries the spider in the ground. When the wasp larva hatches, it slowly eats the paralyzed spider. Since the spider is still alive, its meat stays fresh. Eventually it dies, but by then the wasp larva is ready to turn into an adult wasp.

The caterpillars of cabbage white butterflies are attacked by small black wasps. They may lay 150 eggs in one caterpillar. The tiny wasp larvae feast on the living caterpillar, then pop out and start turning into adults just as the caterpillar finally dies.

This caterpillar has been eaten alive by the larvae of a parasitoid wasp. The larvae are emerging from the caterpillar to turn into adults.

Servants and Slaves

Some **parasites** live in the nests of other animals, and take what they need while their **hosts** do all the hard work. The caterpillars of the European large blue butterfly produce a sweet syrup that ants love to eat. If the ants find a caterpillar they pick it up and carry it home. Once inside the ants' nest, the caterpillar starts eating the ant **larvae**. It produces a special scent that keeps the ants from attacking it, and the ants let it feed on their young until it leaves the nest as a butterfly.

This caterpillar of a large blue butterfly is living among ant larvae. The caterpillar invites ants to take it into their nest, then eats their young.

Slavemakers

In most ant nests, all the eggs are laid by a single queen ant and cared for by hundreds of worker ants. The queen is the mother of all the workers, who build the nest and gather food. But some types of ants called slavemakers do not have normal workers. Instead, they take over the nests of other types of ants, kill their queens, and replace them with their own. Then they get all the workers to look after them like slaves.

Deep in the ocean, the female deep sea anglerfish makes a slave of her mate. The male is tiny compared to the female. When they meet, the male attaches himself to the huge female with his teeth. His body becomes **fused** with hers, and she tows him around to **fertilize** her eggs.

This female anglerfish has two tiny males attached to her back. They cannot feed on their own, so they get all their food through her.

Cuckoos in the Nest

The most famous nest invaders are cuckoos. Some types of cuckoo raise their own young in the usual way, but many lay their eggs in the nests of other birds and expect them to do the parenting. American cowbirds do the same thing. Cuckoos and cowbirds are called **brood parasites.**

A cuckoo watches other birds carefully to see when they lay their eggs. When they leave the nest, she steals one of their eggs and lays one of her own in its place. Although the cuckoo egg is slightly bigger, its pattern matches the others so that the nest owners do not notice the change. The cuckoo, however, has already flown away to lay another egg in a different nest. She may lay up to 25 eggs, all in different nests.

A hungry cowbird chick is stealing all the food brought to the nest by a wood thrush. The thrush's own chicks are likely to starve.

When the baby cuckoo hatches, it pushes all the other eggs out of the nest. This means that it can eat all the food that the adult birds bring. The cuckoo often grows much bigger than the adults, but they keep feeding it until it is ready to fly away.

An adult reed warbler looks tiny next to the giant cuckoo chick that has taken over its nest and destroyed its eggs.

One of the **species** of big, furry bumblebees that you see feeding on flowers is also a brood parasite. It is called the cuckoo bee, because it lays its eggs in the nests of other bumblebees. When they hatch, the cuckoo bee **larvae** are fed and looked after by all the other busy bees, just as if they were their own.

Plant Pests

Most plants make their own food, so they do not have to steal it. A green substance in their leaves, called chlorophyll (klor-oh-fill), soaks up sunlight and uses the sun's energy to turn air and water into sugar. This process is called photosynthesis (foh-toh-sin-thu-sis).

But some plants do not have any chlorophyll and cannot make sugar. They include the ghost orchid, a pale, woodland flower with no green leaves. The orchid attaches itself to an underground fungus. The fungus gathers food from dead and rotting leaves, and the orchid steals some of the food from the fungus to make its own stems and flowers. It is a **parasite.**

Because it does not need light, this strange ghost orchid lives mainly underground. It can survive for years without flowering.

Fungus and plant links

A fungus is not a plant. Like animals, it cannot make its own food. Most fungi feed on dead things. But a few are parasites, like the honey fungus, which attacks the roots of living trees and produces honey-colored mushrooms.

Honey fungus feeds on living plants and eventually kills them. It can spread over huge areas and destroy whole gardens.

The slender orange threads of this dodder plant have tangled around heather stems to steal their sap. The dodder plant uses this food to make its pink flowers.

Sapsuckers

Other plant parasites attack green plants, and steal the sugary fluid called **sap**. One of these parasites is called the dodder plant. It has no green leaves, and it looks like pale orange spaghetti. It crawls over other plants in search of thick, juicy stems. When one of its spaghetti-like **tendrils** finds a stem, it wraps around it and sucks out the sap.

One of the most interesting plant parasites lives in **tropical** Borneo and Sumatra. This parasite, called rafflesia (ruh-flee-zhee-uh), lives inside a rainforest vine. Sometimes a big lump appears on the vine's bark, and a huge, nasty-smelling, orange rafflesia flower bursts out. The rafflesia flower can grow as large as three feet (one meter) across, making it the biggest flower in the world.

Climbers and Stranglers

Green plants need light to make their own food. But in forests, huge trees often block out the light. So smaller plants often find ways of getting above the trees, up in the sunshine. One way for them to do this is to climb up the trees. Another way is to grow from seeds that are often dropped on the branches of trees by birds. These plants are called **epiphytes** (epp-uh-fytes).

orchid and bromeliad links

Many beautiful **tropical** orchids and bromeliads (bro-meal-ee-ads) are epiphytes. They have roots that grip the tree bark, but they do not take anything else from the tree and they do not cause it any harm. Orchids spread roots over tree branches or dangle them in the air to collect water and food. Bromeliads grow in the pockets of wet leaf mold that collect in the hollows of branches. The leaves of many bromeliads form bowls that collect the water and food the plant needs.

Many rain forest orchids live as epiphytes. They get all the water they need from the warm, moist, tropical air.

Although they look like a mass of cobwebs, the Spanish moss that grows on trees in the warmer parts of North and Central America is a type of epiphytic bromeliad.

Stealing water

Some epiphytes, however, are also **parasites**. They include mistletoe, whose sticky seeds get wedged into small holes in bark. The seeds sprout roots that grow into the tree and steal its liquid **sap**. Mistletoe has green leaves that can make their own sugar, but they depend on trees for all their water.

Trees can survive for years with mistletoe growing on them, but some epiphytes are more deadly. The tropical strangler fig sprouts from a seed high in the branches of a tree, but it grows long roots that find their way down the tree trunk to the ground. The roots weave together and cover the tree. They take the water from the ground below the tree, and block out the light from its leaves. In time the tree dies, but the strangler fig survives.

*The deadly roots of this strangler fig have almost hidden the trunk of its **host** tree, which will eventually die and rot away.*

Thieves and Pirates

All **parasites** steal from other living things and give nothing back. Most of them do it secretly, but some animals are open thieves. They are called **kleptoparasites.** *Klepto* comes from the Greek word meaning "thief."

Stealing a meal is nearly always easier than catching your own, but it can also be risky. On the African grasslands, spotted hyenas regularly steal dead animals that a lion has killed. Lions are much bigger than hyenas, but the hyenas travel in big family groups and they usually outnumber the lions. However, roaming groups of lions also steal from hyenas.

A family of spotted hyenas trails a lion carrying a dead wildebeest it has killed. If they get the chance, the hyenas will grab the wildebeest for themselves.

A frigate bird (top) tries to steal a meal of fish from a red-billed tropicbird and save itself the trouble of catching its own food.

Air attack

Hyenas and lions steal food when they have the chance, but some seabirds have become expert pirates. The long-winged frigate birds that nest on **tropical** islands watch for other seabirds returning to their nests with fish. Then the frigate birds attack in midair, scaring the seabirds into dropping their catches. The frigate birds then swoop down to snatch the food before it hits the sea.

A large, powerful gull called the great skua does the same thing to seabirds that fish in the colder waters of the north Atlantic Ocean. It will even attack a gannet, which is bigger than a skua. If the gannet does not drop its catch right away, the skua will seize its tail or one of its wings to knock it off balance. The skua hangs on until the gannet lands on the sea, and will not let go until it gets ahold of the gannet's food.

Fact File

Bubonic plague, a disease that is carried by some bloodsucking fleas, has killed millions of people. In 1348, it spread throughout Europe and killed 25 million people. It was called the Black Death. In 1665, the Great Plague of London killed about 100,000 people. In 1892, bubonic plague swept through Asia and killed over twelve million people. About 2,000 people still catch bubonic plague each year. Luckily, it can now be cured.

Over 10,000 worms have been found in the **intestine** of just one grouse (a bird like a small chicken), and 988 fleas on one guinea pig. The nest of one small bird called the great tit contained 3,469 bugs of one kind or another, and most of them were **parasites**.

The valuable pearls that are found in oysters and mussels are often formed around the eggs of parasitic worms. The oyster or mussel senses the egg and covers it in the substance that makes the pearl, so the egg cannot hatch.

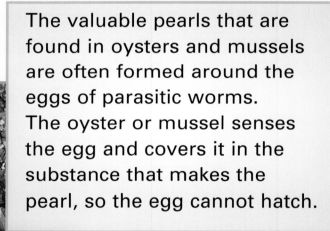

Most parasites live on just one type of animal, or even one part of it. Because of this, there are many, many different types of parasites, each living in a slightly different way. For example, there are about 8,500 different types of birds, but about 25,500 different types of feather lice that live on them.

Scientists have discovered a honey fungus in Michigan that covers an area of at least 149,500 square yards (125,000 square meters). That is much bigger than the biggest dinosaur or whale that ever lived. This honey fungus is one of the largest living things on earth.

The giant tapeworms that live in the intestines of animals are made up of hundreds of sections. New sections grow just behind the creature's head all the time, making it longer and longer. As the sections get older they fill up with eggs, and finally break off at the worm's tail end. It's good for the worm that they break off, because during its life a big tapeworm can produce enough sections so that its body grows up to 4.3 miles (7 kilometers) long!

Glossary

brood parasite   animal that tricks other animals into raising its young

epiphyte   plant that grows in the tops of trees

feces   human body waste

fertilize   to make an egg or seed fertile, so it grows into an animal or plant

fused   when things become joined together so tightly that they become one thing

host   victim of a parasite that lives on the host's body

insect   animal with six legs and three body parts: head, thorax, and abdomen

intestine   long, folded tube attached to an animal's stomach, where its food is digested

kleptoparasite   animal that steals the food from the mouths of other animals

larva (more than one are called larvae)   young insect that does not yet look like its parents. Caterpillars are butterfly larvae.

maggot   legless young flies

paralyze   to damage the nervous system of an animal so it cannot move

parasite   creature that feeds on other living things

parasitoid creature that feeds on other living things and eventually kills them

saliva fluid in an animal's mouth

sap fluid that carries sugar and other substances around plants

species type of living thing

tendril thin, leafless shoot of a plant

tropical describes hot regions of the world where the sun is directly overhead for part of the year

ulcer wound that will not heal

more Books to Read

Houston, Rob. *Feeders.* Chicago: Raintree Publishers, 2003.

Kalman, Bobbie. *What Are Food Chains and Webs?* New York: Crabtree Publishing, 1998.

Martin, James W. R. *Killers.* Chicago: Raintree Publishers, 2003.

McGinty, Alice B. *Scavengers and Parasites in the Food Chain.* New York: Rosen Publishing, 2002.

Index